Foreword

Sheffield is a proud city, and her citizens have much to be proud of. Centuries ago the area was characterised by its isolation from the surrounding towns and countryside - indeed, even the city's name is derived from a word which means *boundary*. It is ironic then, that the more recent history of Sheffield, shaped by enterprise and vision and made possible by outstanding feats of physical labour, usually in difficult conditions, has produced a record of achievement which can only be described as *World class*. This modest book concentrates on the changes that have affected the city centre but includes material relating to social changes and developments which have had an impact on local people. With only one or two exceptions, the common theme throughout the book is concerned with the word *memories*. Photographs have been chosen in the hope that they will bring back the readers' memories of Sheffield, her buildings, streets, shops and transport - hence the title of this book.

It has been said that Sheffield lacks the grandeur of some other northern cities - and critics point to the areas' relatively late development as an industrial town and, again, the isolation and very industrial nature of the commercial success that accompanied her rapid growth. This superficial view of Sheffield does not do justice to the sheer vibrancy of the area - and the passion, ingenuity and northern grit which made the area what it is today. In wartime, industry, sport and many other fields, Sheffield can be proud. In a nutshell, *Sheffield gets on with it,* - and in the future we expect her to do more of the same.

Phil Holland
Publisher.

The Classic Cinema, seen here in 1972

Memories of Sheffield.

First edition published in April 1996 by **True North Holdings**, Dean Clough Industrial Park, Halifax. HX3 5AX.

ISBN
1 900 463 20 2

COPYRIGHT True North Holdings 1996

£4.75

Memories of SHEFFIELD

Contents

Acknowledgements

The late Ron Sanderson, whose excellent pictures feature so strongly in this publication.

Many people have contributed to the content of this book and their assistance is greatly appreciated by the publishers.

The book is based on a collection of photographs from a variety of sources, and most have not been published before. Each of the contributors felt strongly that the photographs in their possession should be seen by a wider audience - and welcomed the idea that fellow Sheffield citizens would share the enjoyment that these pictures bring and the memories which would be rekindled as a consequence. No one expressed this view more strongly than Mrs Maureen Sanderson, widow of the late Ron Sanderson (pictured left) who took most of the contempory photographs in this book. Ron Sanderson was a keen amateur photographer up until his untimely death in 1994, and his dream was always to provide a photographic record of the city he loved. We are pleased to have played our part in realising that ambition for the late Mr Sanderson and his family.

Several pages of *Memories of Sheffield* feature the life of D. C. Marshall and his business The Empire Trading Stamp Company. This gives a fascinating insight to the lives of ordinary Sheffield people and the material was very generously loaned to us by Mrs Dorothy Green and her husband Ivor, of Nether Edge. We are grateful also, to Mr Dennis Askham, of Eckington, for allowing us to use views from his extensive postcard collection. His knowledge and enthusiasm was invaluable for the sections covering the earliest times in the book. Mrs Eileen Hamilton and Mr Norman O'Donnel also lent picture postcards and we must thank them too, along with Mrs Constance Laver who provided examples of work created by her late husband. Aerial photographs were kindly provided from the excellent collection held by Wood Visual Communications of Bradford.

Finally, many thanks to the advertisers who supported the publication of *Memories of Sheffield,* therefore helping to keep the price of the book at a reasonable level. We hope that readers will return this favour by supporting the various businesses concerned.

Three views featuring public transport in Sheffield. The whole of this book could be given over to the fascinating history of Sheffields' transport system - some of the milestones over the years include:

1793:   Sheffield saw the introduction of the first hackney carriages.
1838:   The first horse drawn buses came into service.
        .....and the Railway comes to town.
1873:   Tramlines laid for horse drawn buses.
1877:   Trials took place of steam - drawn buses - they proved unsuitable.
1896:   The Corporation took over the running of the tram system.
1899:   The introduction of the first electric trams.
1902:   Horse drawn trams were phased out.
1911:   Fully enclosed tramcars began service in this year.
1913:   The first Motor Buses were brought into service by the Corporation.
1960:   The last electric trams went out of service.
1992:   ....or so they thought!   ....Supertrams were introduced in Sheffield.

Right: St Paul's Church, with the Town Hall just visible in the background. The lovely building was demolished in 1938 after dominating the site for just over two hundred years. The Peace Gardens are situated on the site now - a welcome area for quiet reflection in the middle of a vibrant city.

Below right : 1909 is the date on the back of this postcard. The location is Wigfull Road - just a stones' throw away from the Botanical Gardens and Hunters Bar. The street looks peaceful enough, but the storm clouds were already gathering which would lead to the start of the First World War just five years later, and change the lives of thousands of Sheffield folk forever.

Below: The date that this scene was captured is unknown, but it is likely to have been either just before, or just after, the turn of the century. The Cutlers Arms - licensee Mr Walker - and The Green Man - landlord Benjamin Wardle - were two popular public houses in this part of the city.

Gripple Limited.

The "West Gun Works" on Savile Street East was built in 1854 by Thos. Firth & Sons to house two new steam hammers. Amongst the earlier guns to be built there were small mountain cannon for the British Government, but by 1871 the company had become one of the best known gun forging firms in the world, employing 1000 men.

The "West Gun Works" became the centre of the Forgemasters' Forged Rolled Mills' until 1991 when the building was subject to a compulsory purchase order by the Sheffield Development Corporation as part of the Lower Don Valley regeneration. In 1994, Gripple Limited took over the restoration of the listed building which was completed in less than six months. Since then it has been the home of "System Gripple", who manufacture a unique range of wire and wire rope joiners for customers worldwide and become a 20th century success story.

Left: This picture, dating from 1899, gives a rare insight to the huge task associated with laying the miles of tram lines for the then modern transport system. The first tramway had been in operation for over 25 years at this time, though the tramcars had been drawn by horses initially. As electric trams increased, horse drawn tramcars were phased out, the last ones running until 1902.

Below, left : Elephant power! This logical approach to the task of transporting heavy metal objects was adopted by Thomas W Ward Ltd of the Albion Works. The firm was known as "Tommy Wards" by most Sheffield folk.

Below: Burngreave Road is pictured here around 1910. The scene is enhanced by the ornate tram standards which typify the era, and the characterful gas lamps which lined the main roads at this time.

Right: Norfolk Hall, a popular food market was situated between King Street and High Street. It was mainly, but not exclusively, a food market and it would have been a familiar and regular shopping haunt of the housewives of Sheffield.

Below, right: Brightside Lane in 1954 had a very different character to the area we see today. Two trams can be seen in this picture - this particular tramway era lasted for another six years, ending in 1960.

Below: This busy scene shows Manor Top in the mid 1950s. The queue at the bus stop and the number of vehicles on the road suggests that the photograph was taken early in the day, with people travelling to work by various modes of transport.

Right: Many Sheffield people will remember an exceptionally tall policeman who used to stand on point - duty at the bottom of High Street for many years. The scene here, looks towards Commercial Street and the year, though unknown, is thought to be sometime in the late 1940s.

Below: A row of trams along King Street - and, quite coincidentally, trams numbers 395 and 396 seen next to each to other when the picture was taken. The Yorkshire Penny Bank building can just about be made out on the right of the picture.

Then and Now....

ANGEL STREET, SHEFFIELD.

216484.J.V.

Above: Waingate, and the Royal Hotel, with Tennant Brothers Exchange Brewery in the background. The tram in the distance is of the open - topped variety - this dates the photograph at between 1899 and 1903.

Above, left: Angel Street at the turn of the century. The building on the left is that famous and much loved department store *Cockaynes*. Ornate tram standards, and, in the distance a fully enclosed tram, complete the picture.

Left: Another view of Angel Street, this time in 1934, but from a similar standpoint. Sadly, this whole area was to be devastated in the German bombings of 1940. Buildings which escaped direct damage from the bombs were gutted by the massive fire which ensued. Cockaynes rose from the ashes, like so many retail establishments which were rebuilt after the war. Sadly though, the name Cockaynes vanished when the company was taken over by Schofields in the early 1970s - and that store closed also, just a decade later.

Above: The massive sign for Wilson Peck and Co. Ltd., dominates this view of City Square. The Cinema House is adjacent to the building and the Victoria Monument can be seen on the left of the picture.

Above right: Another view of Fargate and the Victoria Monument; The Yorkshire Penny Bank occupied the ground floor of the building on the right - the upper floors being the Albany Hotel. Loxley Brothers, the shop with the canopy on the left, was bought by Mrs Viner of the famous cutlery firm, and she turned it into Leonards, the quality dress shop.

Right: Schooldays in the 1930s. This charming picture was sent to us by Mr Harry Kelham of Totley and shows 42 pupils of Maltby Street School posing for their school photo. It is staggering to think that the pupils pictured here will now be at least seventy years of age.

Below: This lovely scene from the late 1950s shows the convergence of three contempory forms of transport at the Wicker Arches. Local people will know that this was the location of the Victoria railway station - opened over hundred years before this photograph was taken, in 1851.

The massive viaduct to carry the railway was completed in 1848. This particular picture is unusual in that it does not show the massive advertising boards which characterised the Wicker Arches for many decades. The motor vehicles on the left are about to travel up the rise in the direction of Spital Hill. The name *Spital* is derived from the word "Hospital" - and this, in this context relates to the St. Leonards Hospital which was established in the area now known as Spital Hill.

Right: The clock in this picture was situated above the building known as the Cabmans Shelter in Fitzalen Square. The building is thought to have been constructed in 1885 - and it was demolished in 1910. Around the bottom of the building benches could be found and this was a popular spot for people waiting for the trams to take them to Brightside and Petre Street.

Amazing but true........

It was said that the construction of the Wicker viaduct - almost 150 years ago - consumed enough stone to build **700** large churches!

Three pictures covering over eighty years in the Darnall area:

Above: This view from around 1912 captures a busy scene at this popular shopping corner. Judging by the long shadow, and the number of men around in the picture, many seen reading the latest edition of the local paper, this could be a Saturday afternoon.

Above, right: In this second picure, from 1952, tramcar number 490 can be seen moving along Staniforth Road, past Main Road and the building occupied by the National and Provincial Bank Ltd. The unusual shallow step in front of the shops on the left of the picture is still there - as is one of the tall iron poles carrying wires across the busy road.

Right: To bring us right up to date - this 1996 photograph, taken from the same location, reveals some interesting changes - as well as some features which have, remarkably, stayed the same. The National and Provincial is now the National Westminster Bank. Smiths Cleaners and The Halifax Building Society are among the popular businesses along Staniforth Road - but that long, shallow step along the shop fronts - and one of the tall iron poles remain in place after all these years.

John Heath & Sons, Funeral Directors

John Heath was born in 1835 and had been in business in Sheffield for a number of years as a Carriage Master, Cabinet Maker and Funeral Undertaker before he established his firm of Funeral Directors in the name of John Heath and Sons in 1880.

At the end of the nineteenth Century John Heath and Sons ran horse drawn omnibus services in and around Sheffield. Before the first World War over a hundred horse drawn vehicles and one hundred and thirty horses were stationed at various mews at Earsham Street, Attercliffe, Walkley, Duke Street, and other branches. At first, Black Belgian horses were used exclusively for funeral corteges and other stately occasions, but John Heaths' son Joseph and his grandson Frank built up a stud of 60 Cleveland Bays. These beautiful animals became known throughout the country, and the Royal Mews bought from John Heath and Sons. At least one of Heath's Cleveland Bays became a Wheeler in the State Coach.

Although a keen and skillful horse breeder, Frank Heath was farsighted enough to be one of the first in the field when cars came on the scene. In the early 1900s John Heath and Sons were agents for Crossley Motors and built car bodies on chassis to order.

The company were agents for Berliet, and later Lea Francis and Singer cars. After the first World War a fleet of taxi cabs was acquired as well as a large fleet of rolls Royce limousines. John Heath and Sons vehicles have always had their own distinctive dark green coachwork, with chauffeurs and bearers dressed in green livery. Limousines are made available for a wide variety of special occasions and, in recent years, the firm has flown the Royal Standard from its Limousines on no less than five occasions.

JOHN HEATH,
CAB PROPRIETOR & GENERAL UNDERTAKER,
SUPPLIES
Wedding and Party Carriages.
FUNERALS FURNISHED
WITH
Glass-Side Hearses or Carved Hearses.
FAMILY SALOON 'BUSES,
AND
SMALL 'BUSES for CHILDREN'S FUNERALS
COFFINS MADE IN THE BEST STYLE.
NOTE ADDRESS
14. EARSHAM STREET—Telephone No. 2029
653. ATTERCLIFFE ROAD
No. 60

Above: John Heath, founder of the company

Above,right: An advert from the 1930s.

..and today

John Heath would be proud of the progress that the company has made since he founded it almost 120 years ago, and impressed by the care which the current management takes in order to preserve the environment by following environmentally sound policies. For example, timber is acquired from sustainable sources which are properly managed and replanted on a "one - for one" basis. Most importantly, the company is at the forefront of promoting the use of environmentally friendly materials in coffin production - particularly for cremation to conform with the new regulations on air pollution control.

Left: This view of Fargate was captured for posterity in the late 1950s, judging by the motor vehicles in the picture. The Timpson shoe shop railings were a popular meeting point for friends going to the Gaumont Cinema - seen on the right of the photograph. Cinemas worked hard to promote forthcoming features - and the Gaumont was no exception. The Gaumont was famous for being the first picture house in Sheffield to show a talking picture. It did so in the year 1929, some two years after it had first opened its doors as the Regent Cinema.

The photographs on the bottom of this and the next page depict elaborate displays which were created by William Edward (known as Ted) Laver in the late 1930s. The pictures were kindly supplied by his widow, Mrs Constance Laver of Beauchief.

Above: The Heeley Electric Palace, on London Road, looks enormous in the photograph from the 1920s. A railway station near Heeley Bridge made it accessible to many people from Sheffield and the surrounding district. The station closed in 1968.

Above, right: The entrance to the Gaumont. Bound to bring back memories to thousands of Sheffield couples of romantic first dates and classic old features. The "alluring autumn attractions" advertised above the doors included "Bulldog Jack" with Jack Hulbert and Clark Gable in "After Office Hours".

Whitbread Plc.

Above: **Bunting and barriers outside Exchange Brewery for the visit of King Edward VII and Queen Alexandra in 1905.**

Right: **A Tennants' Dray at the Exchange Brewery office entrance c1930.**

Below, right: **Tennants' Bottling Plant c1960.**

The company known as Tennants' Brothers moved on to the Exchange Brewery site in 1840 and brewing continued there for around 150 years. At the turn of the century Tennants' Brothers owned more than 100 pubs and off - licences in the city and by the mid 1980s Exchange Brewery was one of the largest traditional breweries in the country.

Whitbread's association with the brewery began in 1953, and in 1961 the two companies merged. Over the years Exchange Brewery produced a wide range of beers, including Wharncliffe Ale, Queen's Ale and Gold Label Barley Wine.

Launched in 1951, Gold Label featured in the Guinness Book of Records as the strongest beer on general sale in the UK.

Below: The year was 1957 when this city centre scene was captured. The Tennants Brewery building can just be made out on the left of the picture, and a close inspection of the building on the right - housing "Thorntons" and Rusbys', reveals a hollow shell behind the facade above the ground floor. This was the year that Harold MacMillan was elected as PM at the age of 62, Britain exploded her first H - bomb, and Stirling Moss achieved a string of land speed records in a tiny 1500cc MG on the Utah Salt Flats in the U.S.A.

Right: This very rare postcard from 1908 depicts the Old Windmill on Attercliffe Common. Little is known about the old mill - which used to stand next to a chimney in the area in the days when the Duke of Norfolk was the Lord of the Manor. Attercliffe itself was a quiet country village up until the early 1800s - and the name *Attercliffe* is derived from words meaning "village at the cliffe".

Memories of SHEFFIELD

Birkdale School.

The two front rooms on the ground and first floors of 9, Newbould Lane were used as the classrooms for the 37 boys who entered Birkdale School after it was established in 1904. Playtime was spent in the back yard, PE was taken in a gymnasium off Clarkehouse Road, and field games were played on a piece of ground at Watt Lane.

Nowadays, with 800 pupils, including Sixth Form girls, and a well established reputation, Birkdale has larger premises and much improved facilities. At nearby Oakholme Road and at the Preparatory School by the Botanical Gardens, the school still retains its family atmosphere and a closely comparable pupil: staff ratio!

The School in 1908, at "Birkdale" in Newbould Lane.

EMPIRE TRADING STAMP COMPANY

This, and the next few pages are devoted to a glimpse into the life and work of a fascinating Sheffield business man, and the thriving local company he created. D.C Marshall was the founder of the Empire Trading Stamp Company, the origins of which can be traced back as far as 1877. The business was initially concerned with the supply of household goods but grew to become a major player in the market for tea, being involved with the wholesaling and retailing side of the business - as well as extensive tea plantations in India and Cylon which were owned by the company.

Marshall was a visionary. He created the trading stamp arm of the business as a way of rewarding the loyalty of his customers - as well as encouraging the growth of his business through his well stocked store at Howard Street. The business began at 23 Howard Street and gradually took over most of the building on that street as trade grew. Most of the company's success occurred in its first twenty years, the peak of its growth coming with the facelift of 19 and 21 Howard Street in 1909.

Above left: The programme from an early staff dinner.
Left: The Howard Street premises in 1921.
Right: Mr D.C. Marshall, pictured in 1909
Above, right: Branch No.3, seen here around 1919

Below: An Empire delivery truck fully decorated to take part in some local procession. The Pride of the Empire theme would have been popular at the time.

Right: An interior view of the Howard Street store in about 1930. Two interesting points; firstly, the rigid looking man on the left is a mannequin - not a customer - and note the lady on the right carrying away her purchases in a brown paper parcel wrapped up with string. A far cry from today's modern packaging.

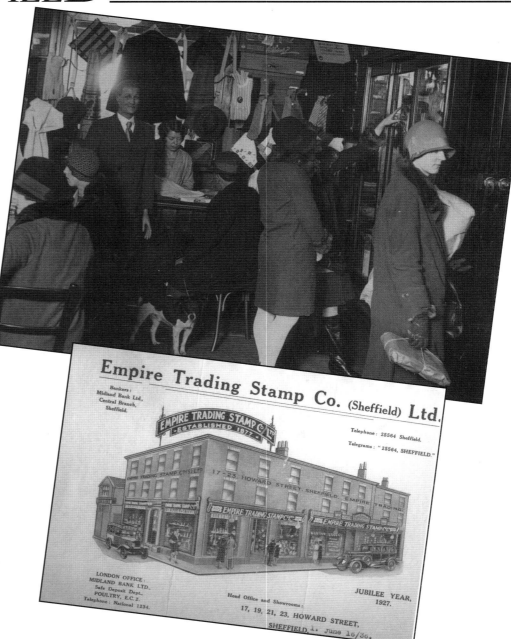

Sheffield Circle of Magicians

Sheffield
Circle
of
Magicians

Founded 1920

President — J. F. BRIDGE, Esq. F.C.I.S.
Past President — R. C. RITSON, Esq. (Wu Ling)

Presents its SIXTEENTH ANNUAL

'Night of Magic'

MONTGOMERY HALL
SURREY STREET   SHEFFIELD

Thursday, November 25th
1937

Curtain 7.30 p.m. prompt

PROGRAMME TWOPENCE

Bingham & Warmby, Ltd., 11-13, Button Lane, Sheffield, 1.

Above: D. C. Marshall, pictured here on the extreme right, and his staff pose for a photograph at the celebrations held to mark the fiftieth anniversary of the company. The year was 1927. At the time of writing, the photograph is almost seventy years old, so it is unlikely that many of the partygoers will have survived long enough to read this book. The year 1927 was notable for at least two achievements which would shape the world; Charles Lindberg made the first non - stop, solo crossing of the Atlantic by air, and, again in America, Al Jolson starred in the first *talking* picture - The Jazz Singer.

Right: D. C. Marshall was enthusiastic about the theatre and entertainment in general. He was very interested in magic - and was a member of Sheffield's Magic Circle for many years. Part of the Marshall business empire involved a theatrical supplies unit and some of the products he supplied are shown here. This stand was constructed for a trade fair in London.

Shopping at the Empire Trading Stamp Company...............

This picture was taken about 1930, and it shows some of the departments inside the premises along Howard Street. It records what it would have been like to shop in store at the time. Interestingly, a close inspection of the young ladies in the photographs reveals some duplication - in other words, the scenes were rather set up - with shop girls pretending to be customers for the photographer!

GRAND PRIZE ANGLING CLUB
(D.C. Marshall's staff)
12 anniversary, September 7 1905.

LEE STEEL STRIP

As every significant town has its Lord Mayor who speaks for the community, Sheffield also has its Master cutler to speak for its industry. City steel company, Arthur Lee and Sons, now known as Lee Steel Strip, has a tradition of providing Master Cutlers, four family members having received this honour.

In 1950, Chairman Wilton Lee had the distinction, and one of his first thoughts was whom he should call to be the principal guest at the Cutlers' Feast to grace and dignify the occasion. Winston Churchill, then leader of Her Majesty's Opposition, who was an ardent supporter of the independence of the steel industry, accepted the invitation. He came, received the freedom of Sheffield and made, in his unique ringing tones, an outstanding speech in praise of the city's steel industry, castigating the government of the day. Recalling the occasion in 1974, Sir Wilton said: "It was a great and proud time to have the old man as my guest, but I tell you... it was the longest 48 hours of my life!" Back to the steelworks.

At the turn of the century, virtually all of the 100 or so employees on Arthur Lee's £160 weekly wage roll were engaged in production; three were in the office, one was a salesman who doubled as wages clerk on Saturday, and one was the gatehouse keeper who clocked in the workers, checked deliveries, worked out piecework rates and weighed the coils of wire. When the company celebrated its centenary in 1974, the company's wages exceeded £30,000 per week.

Above, right: Chairman Wilton Lee meeting Churchill in 1950
Right: Arthur Lee staff pictured in 1900

A November evening in 1974 was chosen to record this dramatic view of Park Square. Many Sheffield residents referred to the large traffic island in the centre of the picture as the "Magic Roundabout" after the popular childrens programme of the time. Dramatic changes have taken place in this part of the city since then, not least of which being the major construction across the roundabout to speed the passage of the latest trams in and out of the centre. The road in the foreground is Bernard Street.

Sheffield

Number one.

Number two

Every photograph on this and the next page was taken by Ronald (Ron) Sanderson. Indeed, most of the *modern* pictures in this book are attributable to him. Born in the Park district of Sheffield in 1944, Ron attended Manor Lodge and Horlfield Secondary Schools where he showed a great talent for art, spending all his spare time drawing and painting, before eventually turning to photography. He achieved an ambition to have a one man exhibition in Graves Art Gallery in the late 1970s. A self taught photographer, his aim was to provide a photographic essay of Sheffield. He was working towards this at the time of his last illness, to which he finally succumed in 1994. His love of Sheffield and the art of photography shows in the quality of his photographs.

Number three

Number four

people!

This selection of eight superb photographs, gives a glimpse of what some aspects of life was like for ordinary people in the Sheffield area. They are only *glimpses* - and they don't pretend to be very much more than that - but the photographs here should do what the rest of the book purports to do - bring back your *memories of Sheffield* and what it was like to live, work and play here over the years.

Number one: "Marvel Boy" Granville Street.
Number two: Workers at George Ibberson,1982.
Number three: Oddfellows Inn Xmas party 1967.
Number four: Salvation Army officer 1971.
Number five: Hard grind at Ibberson's, 1982.
Number six: Customers at the Talbot Inn, 1971.
Number seven: Bill Gibson, Sheaf Island, 1982.
Number eight: Whit Sunday, Talbot Place, 1975.

Number five

Number six

Number seven

Number eight

Left: The Classic Cinema was so named in 1962. It had formerly been the "Wonderland" The Electric Palace and the News Theatre. This picture was taken in 1972, some ten years before it closed it's doors for the last time. A fire in the empty building sealed the fate of the faithful old cinema in 1984. The public house next door is the Bell Hotel, and next to that the Sleep Shop can be seen in this part of Fitzalen Square.

Below: The Park Cinema, situated on South Street, is seen here in 1970. Originally this was the Park Picture Palace, having opened in 1913 under the ownership of Henry Boot and Son. Films were shown here until 1966, prior to an all too familiar conversion to a Bingo Hall.

Right: Town Head Street in 1973. The picture was taken one raw December morning - explaining the absence of traffic and passers-by in the scene. To the right of the picture is the area that will be familiar to most Sheffield people today and known as Orchard Square.

Below: Park Goods Station, from Snow Hill, Hyde Park - viewed here in 1961. The goods yard no longer exists and the area is now occupied by Parkway. In the distance the Netherthorpe Flats dominate the landscape and the keen observer will be able to detect the outline of the well known Victoria Hotel, just right of centre of the picture.

Below: This photograph of the Canal Basin was formerly the Park railway station goods yard. It was taken in 1973. Like so many town and city canals the one near Wharf Street has been the subject of renewed interest recently. The area is currently being renovated
Right: Thought provoking, and typical of the photography of Ron Sanderson, this view of the Sheffield and Tinsley Canal was captured in April 1974. This particular waterway was opened in 1819 - giving Sheffield an outlet to the sea and the trading potential of the rest of the world.

Below: Broad Street Sheffield, and the Industry Inn as it was in 1970. The popular hostelry suffered the same fate as many others at this time - being demolished to make way for road improvements to ease the city's congested streets. The site is now covered by a roundabout.

Right: This fine old building served Sheffield well as the Electricity Board offices at the bottom of Commercial Street. It is pictured here in September 1975 - prior to its demolition to make way for the Ponds Forge swimming complex. Nowadays, the tram viaduct runs up the area on the right of the picture. Much disruption was caused to the roads leading in and out of the City as a consequence of the construction of the modern tramway network in the early 1990s.

This view of Broad Street, looking towards the city centre, dates from 1961. The main road in the foreground is Broad Street itself, and Sheaf Street can be seen running across it in the centre of the picture. The large, darkly imposing building on the right of the scene is the Corn Exchange. A fire in 1947 all but destroyed the building, though it remained as an empty shell until its demolition in 1964.

In the distance, several of the best known, taller buildings in the city can be made out.

Many of the premises along Broad Street remain at the time of writing - including the Magnet Ales public house known as the Old Blue Ball. The biggest change here since the picture was taken is the clearance of the area in the middle of the picture to make way for the Park Square roundabout.

Fred Swallow ran his grocery shop on Talbot Road until it was knocked down in September 1972. Careful examination of the shelves behind the grocer reveals the names of some familiar products. Others, like Parkinsons Blood and Stomach Pills - and *Gay Maid* sugared almonds are rather less well known these days!

This would have been a turbulent time for small independent retailers in the grocery trade - not just in Sheffield, but in the whole of the UK.

The growth in the number of supermarkets, fuelled by low prices and the use of the car to do a weekly shopping trip, resulted in many corner shops going to the wall. Ironically, within 20 years, convenience stores would experience a resurgence in their popularity with the shopping public.

Left: This stark scene from 1976 shows All Saints Church standing alone and defiant after the demolition of surrounding properties in the Pitsmoor area. The Church once claimed to have the highest spire in Sheffield (*note*, not the *tallest*) - due to the already high elevation of the building in relation to other churches in the city. Sadly, All Saints was demolished soon after this picture was taken, though the adjacent school remains in service as a popular community centre.

Below: This *tyreless* delivery bike was rescued from the ruins of Petre Street by these two endearing characters in 1973. Their cheeky faces were captured on camera as they played amongst the discarded relics of the area's previous residents. Sheffield followed the trend set by many towns and cities in the north of England in the 'sixties and 'seventies, clearing vast areas of back to back and terraced dwellings and rehousing the occupants in modern concrete structures. In the event, *Sheffield's* answer to the housing issue was to produce buildings far more radical in design and concept than most of her British counterparts - well intentioned actions which enjoyed varying degrees of success and popularity with their new occupants.

A rare and classic photograph of Sheffield from the air taken in 1947, gives a clear picture of what the city looked like just two years after the end of the Second World War, and only seven years after the city was very badly damaged in the bombing of 1940. Further, widespread changes took place after that time which have largely been concerned with *improvements* to the transport system and redevelopment of the retail heart of the area.

A close up view of the very centre of the city - seen here in 1955. The Town Hall, built between 1891 and 1897, and opened later that year by Queen Victoria, stands imposingly in the centre of the picture. The City Hall can be seen to the right and above - easily recognisable with its' curved rear and standing opposite the War Memorial. The building had been opened some fifteen years earlier in 1932. The Peace Gardens - formerly known as St Paul's Gardens after the church which used to occupy the site, are also clearly distinguishable in this unusually crisp old photograph.

Birds eye view 1961

At the top left of this view the Park goods yard can just about be made out near the Royal Victoria Hotel - and further to the right, the Corn Exchange building which was to be demolished only three years later. Major changes were to take place to this area of the city over the following decade - this would almost certainly be one of the last aerial photographs to capture the appearance of the city before the widespread changes began in earnest.

Birds eye view 1974

By this time, the architecture of the modern industrial and retail premises had begun to dominate the heart of the city, as can be seen from this picture taken from an altitude of 1200 feet. As a reference point, note the Town Hall tower at the top right of the photograph. The open air bus station can be seen on the left of the picture - and the growth in the demands of the motor vehicle is discernable on a dramatic scale.

Few people would have imagined the major changes that would transform the appearance of this part of the city when this scene was captured in 1971. The open air, and very popular Sheaf Market, along with the Electricity Board buildings on the left of the picture, all fell foul of the demolition mens hammer. The open air Sheaf Market was known by Sheffield people as the "Rag and Tag", and most were sad to see this icon of local trading make way for the redevelopment of the area. These days, the land once covered by the Sheaf Market is given up to car parking.

The number 52 bus approaching the junction is travelling down Commercial Street, and the destination is marked Woodhouse.

A thought - provoking picture of "old" and "new" Sheffield in this dramatic scene from 1971. The building just left of centre was the Pond Hill Works occupied by Rodgers Cutlery, prior to its demolition. The area below the balcony, where the photograph was framed, is taken up by the bus station. Just out of view, again below the balcony, is the Penny Black public house, reputed to be the oldest establishment of its kind in the area.

The Park Hill and Hyde Park Flats, rising almost majestically into the sky in the background, were icons of the 1960s housing revolution. Park Hill Flats were opened to their residents in 1961 and Hyde Park Flats followed five years later, the 1300 dwellings becoming home for almost 3,000 residents in 1966. This photograph, worthy of any exhibition, is another of the superb works by the late Ron Sanderson.

Below: Sheaf Market, Broad Street and, again, Hyde Park Flats rising in the background like a film set for a futuristic science fiction movie.

Above: An almost intimate view of Hyde Park Flats, taken from St Johns Road in 1969. At the time this picture was taken the building had been in place for just three years, after being opened by the Queen Mother in 1966.

The Hyde Park housing complex was always seen as the poor relation to the more popular Park Hill complex - and suffered from several technical and social problems. Most people agree that the main advantage of the Park Hill flats over their near neighbours was the fact that each level was joined from the start to ground level by a series of wide decks. This meant that residents were not reliant upon lifts for access to their homes. For whatever reason, the Hyde Park Flats fell into disrepair during the 1980s, therefore drawing a veil over one of the city's less successful housing projects.

Events from 1968.......
* First class stamps were introduced.
* Ireland: the (modern) *Troubles* began
* Martin Luther King was assassinated.
* Prescription charges introduced in UK

Milestones from 1969.......
* Man first set foot on the Moon.
* The voting age was reduced to 18.
* Troops sent into Northern Ireland.
* Colour TV was launched in the UK

Right: Sheffield "from the air" - photographed just over a quarter of a century ago in 1970. The distinctive shape of the Park Hill Flats can be seen in the foreground, on the right. The Sheffield Polytechnic - later to be granted University status, and the bus station in front of it - can be seen slightly left of the centre of the view. On the right, just beyond Castlegate and Bridge Street, the outline of the river Don completes the picture.

Left: Another view of Sheaf Street and the old Sheaf Market - taken in 1971. The construction of the new market is going on in the background - just in front of the Woolworth building.

Left: A rare and impressive aerial photograph dating from 1967. Construction work can clearly be seen at its mid point as the economically vital task of extending the M1 to Leeds was underway. The picture here shows Junction 34 at Tinsley. Easily recognisable landmarks - the twin cooling towers of the Blackburn Meadows Power Station, can be seen in the centre of the photograph. The sports ground near Bawtry Road is shown in the foreground, and the steel works and railway marshalling yard is clearly visible.

This scene from 1961 is guaranteed to bring back memories - perhaps particularly to former regulars of the Durham Ox. Behind that well known watering hole can be seen the Royal Victoria Hotel, adjacent to the Victoria Railway Station. In the distance, construction work is being carried out on the Pye Bank Flats. Their reign over the skyline was fairly shortlived when set against the history of Sheffield - they were demolished around thirty years after this picture was taken.

These days, a tram viaduct for the modern system runs behind The Durham Ox, and the area to the left of the picture is now the subject of extensive renovation around the canal basin.

A dramatic view of quarrying activity taken in 1957. The location is Granville Road - the effect of quarrying can be seen on the right of the main road, on the area known as Clay Wood. On the left of Granville Road Castle College can be seen next to the railway line which runs to Sheffield station, middle right. Above that, the bus station can just be made out, as well as construction work which is taking place on the tall, light coloured building which was to form part of the new Polytechnic.

Slightly left, and above centre, the triangular shape of the Shoreham bus depot, along with rows of double decker vehicles outside it can be discerned. This was opened in 1911 as a tram depot - with a capacity then of no less than 114 tramcars.

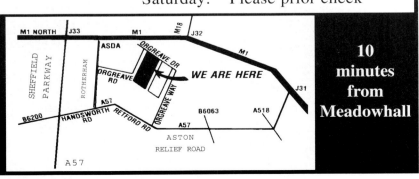
The story of the Cutlery Trade in Sheffield.

Sheffield has been a major player in the Cutlery Industry for more than 500 years. The word *cutlery* has latin origins, being derived from a word which means *knife*. The industry was initially concerned with knife making, for weapons and tools as well as for eating. The trade later grew to take in the production of forks, spoons and razors.

The first mention of Sheffield as a centre for the production of cutlery was in the fourteenth century, in records of goods held at the Tower of London. In 1624 the Company of Cutlers in Hallamshire was formed by around 500 individuals in order to promote and regulate the interests of the Sheffield Cutlers. The industry was boosted over the next 150 years as a consequence of two very important local advantages: Firstly, the availability of a type of sandstone which was very suitable for use in grindstones. This was in turn linked to the second natural advantage which benefited Sheffield cutlers in comparison to their rivals, and this was *water power*. The local, fast flowing rivers and streams could be harnessed to create powered grinding wheels in order to speed up the process of putting a sharp edge on the many products produced by the Cutlers. By 1780 there were over 160 water powered grinding shops in the Sheffield area.

Another milestone in the development of the Sheffield cutlery industry was the invention of *crucible steel*. This was far superior - though initially harder to work - than the previous raw material - and it gave Sheffield a competitive advantage for a further 100 years. The structure of the manufacturing industry concerned with cutlery was unusual in the eighteenth century. Little Mesters were small, independent businesses, usually consisting of two or three skilled workers, who worked for one or two large companies on an "as needed" basis. This gave advantages to both parties - with considerable flexibility and efficiency on both sides. The system encouraged innovation and specialisation with the emphasis on specialist skills in a given, focussed area. The Little Mesters continued to be a significant element in the structure of the Cutlery Industry right up until the end of the 1930s.

Growth continued throughout the eighteenth century - with over 15,000 local workers being involved in the trade by the year 1900 - over twenty times the number employed in London's cutlery trade - where the UK cutlery activity was once centred. The start of the twentieth century saw another important - if not crucial invention for the continued prosperity of the cutlery industry. It was the development of stainless steel by Harry Brearley of Thomas Firth & Sons, in 1913. The critical advantage of stainless steel was that it did n't rust.

Sheffield's cutlery trade was badly affected by the decline in industrial and economic prosperity in the 1970s and 1980s. In line with other industries, the trade suffered from competition from cheap foreign imports and an era where customers appeared to be more interested in price than value. Quality, however, is rarely out of fashion for long, and there is no doubt that the quality for which Sheffield's cutlery has built a worldwide reputation will secure the cutlers' craft well into the next century.

WALTER TRICKETT & Co. SHEFFIELD

A DIVISION OF CHIMO HOLDINGS

The name of Walter Trickett & Co. is associated with the finest hand finished cutlery and known throughout the world. The company was established over 100 years ago and is now part of the Chimo Holdings group of companies. Some of Sheffield's best known small cutlery companies - including Kirkanson and Mottershaw & Rowe, combined with White Rose Silverware to form Chimo Holdings at their Sheffield base on Eyre Lane.

The company is one of the few remaining *cutlers* of its kind because of the way it uses traditional, very labour intensive methods to produce handcrafted goods. Indeed, the business was once featured on a BBC programme entitled *Against the Grain* to illustrate the way that some firms fight the mass production techniques of their competition by achieving very high quality from a skilled and experienced workforce. The other element of the company which really sets it apart from it's rivals, is the use of traditional raw materials in the production area. Bone handles are extensively used - mainly stag and buffalo in origin - and, crucially, all shed naturally by the animals concerned. "Nostalgia" is a superior quality, reproduction bonehandled range of cutlery from yesteryear, still extremely popular today as is the extensive selection of mother of pearl products.

The company produces an amazing range of unusual cutlery pieces, along with all the items you would expect in a Sheffield cutlery factory. Among some of the more unusual items sent around the world are peacock spoons, cranberry ladles, caviar spoons, asparagus tongs and elaborate tea strainers.

Walter Trickett & Co. ensure that the name of *Sheffield* is seen in the most exclusive stores in countries as diverse as Japan, USA, Sweden, E.C countries, Australia and the Caribbean - indeed, the majority of the organisation's production is exported. Chris Hudson - general manager - is proud of the export achievement of the firm, and unashamed of their objective of satisfying the "quality" end of the market for fine, handcrafted cutlery. Many palaces, government offices, banks and hotels throughout the world contain Sheffield cutlery produced by the company - including our own Royal households, handcrafted by his team on Eyre Lane. In doing so the company is playing it's part in maintaining the craftsmans tradition - one which has endured for over 500 years.

.....Tomorrow's heirlooms being handcrafted *today*

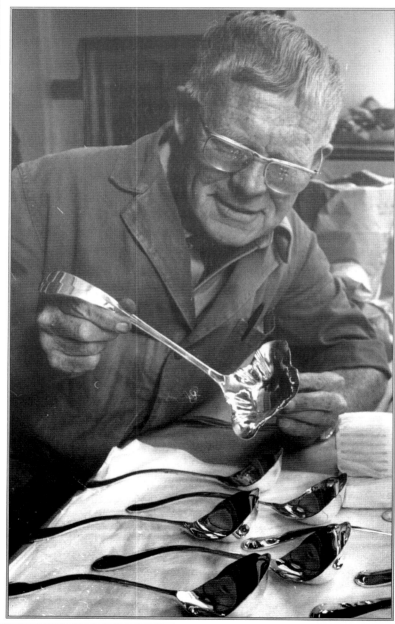

CUTLERY VISITOR CENTRE AND MILL SHOP OPENING MID - 1996

We are pleased to announce the opening of our visitors centre and mill shop in the summer of 1996.

Members of the Guild of Mastercraftsmen since 1990

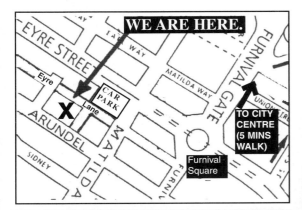

WE ARE HERE.

EYRE STREET
Eyre Lane
CAR PARK
X
ARUNDEL
MATILDA WAY
FURNIVAL GATE
TO CITY CENTRE (5 MINS WALK)
Furnival Square
SIDNEY

White Rose Works, 61 Eyre Lane, Sheffield, South Yorkshire S1 3GF
Tel. 0114 249 0969 *Fax 0114 249 0922*

The Walter Trickett Visitors Centre and Mill Shop will offer a unique opportunity to:

* Watch our ***craftsmen*** actually making quality cutlery by hand.
* See the different processes which are involved for yourself.
* Buy bargains, seconds and souvenirs from our mill shop.
* Ask advice about our resharpening and replating services.
* Conveniently situated within walking distance of the city centre

Organised parties welcome - <u>advance booking essential</u>

Cutlery made on our premises is exported worldwide - and graces the dining tables of many Royal palaces. Come and see our craftsmen, using traditional methods handed down over the centuries, as they produce some of the finest cutlery in the world. We use quality materials in the production of our goods - including buffalo and stag horn (which has been shed naturally by the animals concerned) - plus mother of pearl and the finest gold, silver and stainless steel. Many of these products are available in our mill shop at bargain prices.

***<u>IMPORTANT!</u>** Please phone for details of opening times and availability of guided tours in advance*

> **Thoughts on quality........**
>
> *"It's unwise to pay too much, but it's worse to pay too little. When you pay too much you lose a little money - that is all. When you pay too little, you sometimes lose everything, because the thing you bought was incapable of doing the thing it was bought to do.*
> *The common law of business balance prohibits paying a little and getting a lot - it can't be done.*
> *If you deal with the lowest bidder, it is well to add something for the risk you run.*
> *And if you do that, you will have enough to pay for something better.*
>
> **John Ruskin 1819 - 1900**

WALTER TRICKETT & Co.

A DIVISION OF CHIMO HOLDINGS

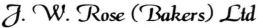